Tassel-Free
Living *for*
Grads

God's Grace for Grads

Tim Wesemann
www.timwesemann.com

www.ctainc.com

Tassel-Free Living
God's Grace for Grads
ISBN 0-9718985-8-8

GREAT!

REGAL!

AWESOME!

DISTINGUISHED!

UNSURPASSED!

ASTOUNDING!

TREMENDOUS!

EXCELLENT!

Sit for a SPELL and read the
rave reviews about your graduation!

Congratulations and future blessings!

The L̲ORD̲
has done great things
for us, and we are
filled with *joy.*

~ *Psalm 126:3*

THIS IS THE DAY THE LORD HAS MADE;
LET US REJOICE AND BE GLAD IN IT.

~ *Psalm 118:24*

Table of Contents

Rejoice in the LORD always. *I will say it again:* **Rejoice!**

~Philippians 4:4

Congratulations!

You *just turned,* or are about to turn, the tassel on your mortarboard, signifying that you've officially completed the work required for graduation! The turn of the tassel also means that you have turned to a new chapter of your life—life beyond graduation.

The days surrounding graduation are filled with questions, excitement, and even some anxiety. But perhaps, too, they are filled with reflection— reflection on some of the blessings God has given you over the past years.

It's interesting to think about how God uses people, places, and experiences to shape and mold us, to form us into the people he wants to use as his ambassadors to the world. Who and what has God used to fill your days these past few years with blessing and growth? In the back of this book, you will find a journal where you can record those people, places, and experiences. Then in the future you can return to them for moments of reflection and encouragement.

continued on next page

praise

Your past plays a big part in your future. The same God who has held you in his hands all along your way also holds your future. He has great plans for you. He wants you to seek out his will for your life each day, no matter what your age or situation. Even though the coming months and years will bring many changes, the promises and love of your God through his Son Jesus will never change. That truth is the greatest graduation gift ever given. And it's a gift that will affect you every day of your life.

> *After graduation, you can live "tassel-free," but you will rarely live hassle-free.*

Graduation is a high note in a life that, like all lives, will have highs and lows. After graduation, you can live "tassel-free," but you will rarely live hassle-free. The hassles you face might be temptations from Satan, the result of your own or others' personal choices, or simply the after-shock of living in a world separated from God by the sin of the people around you.

As you hit those high and low notes, remember to rely on God's grace, the undeserved love of your Savior, Jesus Christ. In the midst of both high notes and low notes, a close relationship with Jesus will turn your future into a beautiful and adventurous present, a real song of praise.

So, again,

congratulations!

And God's blessings on each day of your new life!

promises

If you think *education. is expensive,* try *ignorance*

~Andy McIntyre

TO THE UNEDUCATED,
AN A IS JUST THREE STICKS.

~A.A. Milne

Pomp and Circumstance

in the Key of Aaaayyy!

If you're a fan of television reruns, you may know about the character Fonzie from the show *Happy Days*. As the king of cool, his calling card phrase for this show, set in the 1950's, was "Aaaayyy!" With this expression, he would throw out his chest, tilt his head, and give a "thumbs up" sign. Fonzie projected the image of a cool, proud, and in-control young man. After all, he was Fonzie! The women loved him, his friends stood in awe of him, and enemies feared him!

The word "pomp" comes from a Greek word, meaning a solemn procession, a stately display.

Lots of pomp surrounds the circumstance of most graduations. In fact, school bands or orchestras usually play the song "Pomp and Circumstance" as graduates walk to their seats at the beginning of the graduation ceremony.

The word "pomp" comes from a Greek word, meaning a solemn procession, a stately display, splendor, or magnificence. And the word "circumstance" is from the Latin word circu, which means "to stand." It refers to the ceremony or the conditions that surround and affect a person.

Circumstances in our lives can make us stronger, or we can allow them to hinder us. Have you considered the circumstances that brought you to a pomp-filled event called graduation?

The composer of "Pomp and Circumstance," Edward Elgar, had many unusual circumstances —highs and lows—in his life. He was a self-taught genius who received great acclaim for his musical gifts, but tragically suffered from attacks of prejudice, cancer, and depression, and spent five years serving as an unappreciated, ridiculed bandmaster in a county asylum for those enduring mental illness. "Pomp and Circumstance" expresses his conflicting feelings of triumph and failure, creating an underlying strain of nostalgia to which we can all relate. This makes the piece uniquely suited to the ceremonies that mark the end of one stage in life and the beginning of the next.

You have achieved something worth celebrating. So enjoy!

Walking down the aisle at graduation can create that Fonzie-like "Aaaayyy" feeling. I'm a graduate! Tassel-free living is mine! I'm the top dog, king of the hill! People will stand in awe of me!"

rejoice!

You have achieved something worth celebrating. So enjoy! But at the same time, be careful! Beware of Fonzie-itus! Don't become puffed up with sinful pride. Rejoice in your accomplishment! Celebrate your graduation! But remember, there are two kinds of pride. One grows from an appropriate satisfaction that honors God for all he has done. The other

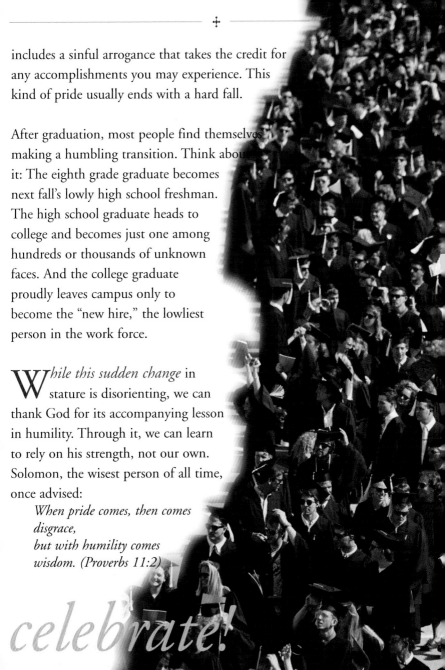

includes a sinful arrogance that takes the credit for any accomplishments you may experience. This kind of pride usually ends with a hard fall.

After graduation, most people find themselves making a humbling transition. Think about it: The eighth grade graduate becomes next fall's lowly high school freshman. The high school graduate heads to college and becomes just one among hundreds or thousands of unknown faces. And the college graduate proudly leaves campus only to become the "new hire," the lowliest person in the work force.

While this sudden change in stature is disorienting, we can thank God for its accompanying lesson in humility. Through it, we can learn to rely on his strength, not our own. Solomon, the wisest person of all time, once advised:

> When pride comes, then comes disgrace,
> but with humility comes wisdom. (Proverbs 11:2)

celebrate!

Though this is an exciting and proud time in your life, ask God to build into your heart the great wisdom of humility. Enjoy the blessings of graduation, but realize that without God's gifts, you would not have made it to this point.

This is what the Lord says:

"Let not the wise man boast of his wisdom or the strong man boast of his strength or the rich man boast of his riches, but let him who boasts boast about this: that he understands and knows me, that I am the LORD, who exercise kindness, justice, and righteousness on earth, for in these I delight," declares the LORD.

(Jeremiah 9:23-24)

St. Paul echoes Jeremiah's words and goes a step further:

May I never boast except in the cross of our Lord Jesus Christ, through which the world has been crucified to me, and I to the world.

(Galatians 6:14)

Heyyyyy! You're a graduate!

Congrats!

Yeaaaa!

You're a graduate!

Blessings!

humili

Aaaayyy! You're a graduate! Humbly take the pomp and boast in the Lord who gifted and guided you to achieve your accomplishment through circumstances of his design!

Aaaayyy! You're a graduate! Graciously and boldly step forward as the Lord leads you. Know that he goes ahead of you and will continue to bring circumstances together for your good, shaping you into the person he wants you to become!

Heyyyyy!
Yeaaaa!
Aaaayyy!
You're a graduate!

Congratulations!

May God continue to bring out HIS best in you as you live for him, whatever the circumstances, whatever the pomp!

T_herefore, as God's chosen people,_ holy and dearly loved, clothe yourselves with compassion, kindness, humility, gentleness, and patience. Bear with each other and forgive whatever grievances you may have against one another. Forgive as the Lord forgave you. And over all these virtues put on love, which binds them all together in perfect unity.

Let the peace of Christ rule in your hearts since as members of one body you were called to peace. And be thankful. Let the word of Christ dwell in you richly as you teach and admonish one another with all wisdom, and as you sing psalms, hymns and spiritual songs with gratitude in your hearts to God. And whatever you do, whether in word or deed, do it all in the name of the Lord Jesus, giving thanks to God the Father through him.

~ Colossians 3:12-17

patience

The fireworks begin today.
Each diploma is a
lighted match.
Each one of you
is a fuse.

~Ed Koch

I pray that out of [Christ's] glorious riches [God]
may strengthen you with power through
his Spirit in your inner being,
so that Christ may dwell
in your hearts through faith.
And I pray that you, being rooted and
established in love, may have power,
together with all the saints, to grasp how wide
and long and high and deep is the love of Christ,
and to know this love that surpasses knowledge—
that you may be filled to the measure of all
the fullness of God.

Now to him who is able to do immeasurably
more than all we ask or imagine,
according to his power that is at work within us,
to him be glory in the church and in
Christ Jesus throughout all generations,
for ever and ever! Amen.

~ Ephesians 3:16-21

Jesus Loves Me

in the Key of Be!

During the time you spent in school, you learned plenty of facts, figures, rules, and exceptions to rules. You completed projects and lab reports, read books that piqued your interest and some that put you to sleep. You thought some assignments were easy, yet never fully understood others. Your writing was mediocre on certain days and brilliant on others!

There's been . . .
Math.
English.
History.
Geography.
Spelling.
Music.
Literature.
Science.
Foreign Languages.
Physical Education.

Do you remember all the classes?
Do you remember everything
you learned?

Do you remember all your teachers?
Do you remember all the notes you took?

It's probably safe to say you don't remember all the details of the education you received. And it's also probably safe to say there were times you didn't want to remember the details because they lacked relevance to your life— your interests and dreams.

> *Another goal your teachers had when introducing all those seemingly irrelevant details concerns your career path.*

However, one of the goals your teachers had was to lay a strong foundation for your journey through life, not just your place in life. They desired to contribute to your personality, friendships, and emotions with a well-rounded education that, in turn, might help you shape the lives of everyone you encounter in your future, not just those who are identical to you or those who share your same interests and dreams. A well-rounded education prepares you to be God's instrument in a multi-hued world of varied interests and diverse dreams.

Another goal your teachers had when introducing all those seemingly irrelevant details concerns your career path. For example, how many times over

planning

someone ask you, "What do you want to be when you grow up?" (Or, in some cases, "… when you finally grow up"!) The answers you gave to that question may have changed more often than the seasons of the year. Studying many topics helps you see career paths beyond those you might encounter in everyday life.

> *Your teachers also knew that all we learn contributes to all we become.*

Your teachers also knew that all we learn contributes to all we become. They presented endless details to ponder, absorb, reject, and examine because the process of doing so adds depth to who we are. In fact, some of the facts you learned in early elementary school are still a big part of you. For instance, knowing it's important to spell korrectly (ah, make that "correctly") sticks with you as you complete college or move on to fill out job applications. And, the simple addition and subtraction you first learned in elementary arithmetic plays a huge part in the shopping, planning, and building you're doing today. Does math and spelling seem irrelevant to life as a second grader? Sure! (Anything separate from recess seems irrelevant to a second grader.) Still, everything you learned in second grade has helped to shape you into the person you've become.

Among all the details to be learned is one most critical detail, the greatest, deepest, and most significant truth in all of life. It might seem irrelevant or insignificant in its simplicity, but it matters for a lifetime more than anything else you have learned or will learn:

> *Jesus loves me this I know*
> *For the Bible tells me so!*
> *Little ones to him belong*
> *They are weak, but he is strong!*

When you die, it won't matter how many master's degrees you have earned. But if you realize the degree of love the Master, Jesus, has for you, it will make an eternal difference.

In Jesus Christ you will find your foundation, your life, your all. Even in your weakness you will find strength—his strength.

The greatest mathematical equation:
1 Savior on a cross + 3 nails = 4-giveness

The greatest history lesson:
His-story.

The greatest and most current geopolitical statement:
I am the way and the truth and the life.
No one comes to the Father except through me.

(John 14:6)

The greatest piece of profound literature, penned under the inspiration of the Holy Spirit:
the Bible.

When you die, it won't matter how many master's degrees you have earned.

Because the Bible tells you that Jesus loves you, you realize your life has meaning and purpose. You are not just a number. You aren't just another body taking up space on this planet.

You are a dearly loved, forgiven child of God, created with a unique purpose in his kingdom. He knew and loved you before he created the world. God—Father, Son, and Holy Spirit— created you to BE!

You will find the key to that BE-ing in Jesus Christ, your Savior. In him you find your hope and purpose. Allow him to continue to teach, mold, shape, and form you. Look for the details of his life and make them the details of your own.

And the next time someone seriously (or jokingly) asks you what you want to be when you grow up, smile and say, "I already am what I am always going to be—a dearly loved, forgiven child of God!"

Class dismissed!

Go into the world knowing that

YOU ARE LOVED!

I have
never let
my schooling
interfere with
my education.

~Mark Twain

THERE IS A GOOD REASON
THEY CALL THESE CEREMONIES
"COMMENCEMENT EXERCISES."
GRADUATION IS NOT THE END; IT'S THE BEGINNING.

~ Orrin Hatch

*Grace and peace to you from God our Father
and the Lord Jesus Christ.
I always thank God for you because of his grace
given you in Christ Jesus ...
He will keep you strong to the end,
so that you will be blameless on the day of
our Lord Jesus Christ.
God, who has called you into fellowship
with his Son Jesus Christ our Lord, is faithful.*

~ 1 Corinthians 1:3-4, 8

✝

May our LORD Jesus Christ himself
and God our Father,
who loved us and by his grace gave us
eternal encouragement and good hope,
encourage your hearts and
strengthen you in every good deed and word.

~ *2 Thessalonians 2:16-17*

Amazing Grace

in the Key of Gee!

There was a girl in my school named Grace. She was amazing! She seemed to 'ace' every subject. That amazed me, especially when I compared her report card to mine! We could take the same classes, but her results were always better than mine. I'd scratch my head in bewilderment and think, "Gee, Grace is amazing!"

The hymn "*Amazing Grace*" wasn't written about the girl who attended school with me. The grace to which the song refers is a word that means "undeserved love."

> *The grace to which the song refers is a word that means "undeserved love."*

God's love is amazing! Why would the Creator of the entire universe care about every aspect of our lives? Because he's amazing! Why would he kill his own Son on a cross to cancel out every self-centered thought or action in us—just so we can live forever in his light, under his protection, within his comforting arms? Because he's amazing! Think of all his many other gifts of love and life—all are undeserved. Life with him is truly amazing! Nothing we have done or will do can earn for us God's forgiveness and salvation; instead, both are freely given to us through Jesus Christ. What an amazing God!

be mine

＋

This widely-used acronym for the word grace helps explain what it means:

grace

G-od's
R-iches
A-t
C-hrist's
E-xpense

Grace is God's riches at Christ's expense. Our Savior, Jesus Christ, gave his life so that all the riches of heaven could be ours: forgiveness, hope, peace, eternal life, and all of God's other, many blessings.

When stripped to its core, our nation's system of education, including the process of graduation, is based on rules. Those in authority grant rewards and apply penalties according to how a student responds to those rules.

For example, students must complete a certain number of assignments during a specific time period. When students turn in those assignments, they receive a grade based on how well they followed the guidelines, or rules, of the assignment. In other words, do this, and you receive a reward—a passing grade. Don't do it, or do it poorly, and you do not receive the reward. If you don't collect enough rewards, you do not graduate.

$\dagger$

Y*ou've lived within this structure* for several years. If you continue to the next level of schooling, you will encounter this same structure again. But even if you leave school for the work force, you will have to continue living within it. For in the work force, your supervisor will assign work, probably with deadlines. If you complete that work satisfactorily, you will receive a paycheck as a reward. If you don't, or if you produce poor results, you will be disciplined or even fired. Rules to live by and rewards to hope for—it's a way of life in this world.

> *Rules to live by and rewards to hope for—it's a way of life in this world.*

But God's world of grace works in quite a different way! Don't confuse the structure of life in this world with life in God's universe of grace.

There is no possible way anyone could come close to receiving a passing grade in God's school or acceptable results in God's employment. You see, he demands 100% perfection. Anything less than that is failure: But whoever keeps the whole law and yet stumbles at just one point is guilty of breaking all of it (James 2:10).

These demands don't leave room for much hope! Who can be perfect?

rewards

And yet, if we break any of God's laws, we have failed. That's right, a big fat "F" on the report card of our lives.

Jesus lived a perfect life in our place — in your place!

FSo what do we do? We have to take our report card home and show it to our heavenly Father. Will he willingly sign it when we have received failing marks in every aspect of our lives?

Check out this amazing, good news for everyone—for you, too, whether you ace every subject or your grades are less than spectacular.

Our heavenly Father has already signed the report card for your life. He signed it in blood—the blood of his Son, Jesus. You see, Jesus lived a perfect life in our place—in your place!

Not only did he live a perfect life, he willingly sacrificed himself on the cross to take the punishment for our imperfect lives. He took away all our sins, suffering all of the heavenly Father's anger, anger that we deserved! Jesus died—and we live! We sin, and he forgives! We fail, but he gives us an A+ as well as extra credit for the work he did! We don't deserve any of it, but it's all ours as a free gift.

These are amazing gifts, amazing gifts of grace! And this grace changes the way we live—on earth, and one day in heaven!

God's grace turns the world's way of doing things upside down! The world will continue shouting about its rules and rewards. That's just the way the world works, and, for now, we live in this world. But at the same time, those who know Jesus live under the amazing grace of God. And what a great place that is to live!

You may plan to continue your education after graduation, or you may move into the work place. Whatever your plan, remember that even if someone named Grace sits next to you, acing everything in sight, you have received an ocean of truly amazing grace in your Savior, Jesus. Don't just get that fact into your head. Get it into your heart, and let it change your life eternally!

GRACE!
AMAZING!

AMAZING GRACE!

WHAT A WAY OF LIFE!

At commencement you wear your **square-shaped mortarboards.** *My hope is that from* **time to time** *you will let your minds be* **bold,** *and wear* **sombreros**

~ Paul Freund

Open the Eyes of My Heart

in the Key of See!

Graduation is a time of anticipation ...
When your eyes are filled with stars (and maybe some tears), it's hard to focus on what's going on around you.

Too many times, big moments in our lives pass us by.

Too many times, big moments in our lives pass us by. We forget to really take in everything, to store it solidly in our memory bank. Ask some couples about their weddings, and they can't remember many specifics about the day because so much activity swirled around them.

It's the same way with graduation. Crowds form, people hug you, friends say good-by, teachers congratulate you, your family wants your attention, the commencement speakers talk, a dignitary distributes diplomas, you turn your tassel and send your mortarboard flying into the sky. So much goes on!

focus

It'll be like that for the rest of your life. We live in a fast-paced world. Computers, cell phones, cars, televisions, radios, people crying out for attention, hectic work schedules, parties, commitments to family and friends… the list goes on and on.

Still, God's blessings fall like constant rain from heaven. These blessings come in:

☩ 24-hour pizza delivery during finals or a smile delivered with a college acceptance letter (finally!);

☩ the significant turning of a word or the signifying turn of a tassel;

☩ expected kisses from grandma or unexpected hugs from classmates;

☩ encouraging words from a friend that surprisingly fill your heart with courage;

☩ God's quiet answer following a time of quiet prayer;

☩ the Father's holy presence as well as his holy present: a Savior named Jesus.

Too many times, big moments in our lives pass us by.

The list is endless! God's gifts blanket our lives. Don't be blinded by the glare of selfishness or the glitz of the world. Slow down! Take a look around! You don't want to miss God's world of blessings all around you!

Pray, "Open the eyes of my heart, Lord. I want to see! I want to see you! I want to see your blessings . . . and to live a life of thanksgiving in response to it all."

Then enjoy the sights beyond the tassel that hung in front of your eyes at graduation! And don't forget to thank God for all of them!

Don't be afraid to take a *big step* if one is indicated; *You* can't cross a chasm in *two small* jumps.

~David Lloyd George

A FELLOW TOLD ME HE WAS GOING TO HANG-GLIDER SCHOOL.
HE SAID, 'I'VE BEEN GOING FOR THREE MONTHS.'
I SAID, 'HOW MANY SUCCESSFUL JUMPS
DO YOU NEED TO MAKE BEFORE YOU GRADUATE?'
HE SAID, 'ALL OF THEM.'

~ Red Skelton

[Jesus said,] "Do not be afraid, little flock,
for your Father has been pleased
to give you the kingdom."

~ Luke 12:32

[Jesus said,] "Peace I leave with you;
my peace I give you.
I do not give to you as the world gives.
Do not let your hearts be troubled
and do not be afraid."

~ John 14:27

[The LORD Says,]
"For I am the LORD, your God,
who takes hold of your right hand
and says to you,
Do not fear; I will help you."

~ Isaiah 41:13

Fear Not, Little Flock

in the Key of Eeeeee!

The graduation ceremony has ended; the guests have left. You've opened all the gifts and thrown away the wrapping paper. The school doors are locked. Now you're lying in bed, holding your graduation tassel in your hands.

> *You need not approach the future in fear.*

It's definitely time to take the next step. The past is past. Your history has shaped you, but the future lies ahead. It's time to live tassel-free, but what hassles lie hidden ahead? As you think about it, you may want to belt out a fearful "Eeeeee!" But you need not approach the future in fear. You may be in for a more exciting ride than you've ever dreamed possible!

Yes, life is tough. People can be heartless. No doubt plenty of challenges lie ahead of you in life beyond the graduation tassel. But as you head into an unknown future, remember that you step out with your well-known God leading the way. You know him, and he knows you. Not only that, he also knows each of your concerns, struggles, temptations, and fears.

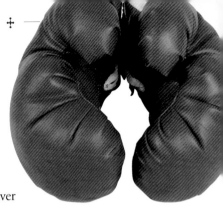

God is on your side. He's in your corner. He loves you and covers you with the blood-bought blessings of his Son, Jesus. Here are some truths that can give you an amazing confidence—in Christ—to walk boldly into any and every situation. Read and re-read these truths whenever you need encouragement:

1   ***Your Savior has equipped you through the events and education*** of the past to handle any future situation.

2   ***God has gifted you with teachers, mentors, parents, and friends*** to whom you can turn when you need help in facing struggles or making decisions. Look to them for support. Rely on them for counsel, but don't compare your situation or life to theirs; everyone has different gifts, experiences, and life situations. You are unique, and so is your situation.

unique

3 ***Turn to God's Word for help.*** Scripture can answer so many of life's questions! It's not out-dated. Rather, it is your best guide for living the abundant, forgiven, and eternal life Jesus has planned for you. Pray over the words of Scripture for wisdom and grace as you seek God's will.

4 ***Rely on the calling your Lord has placed on your life.*** You are a child of God. You are saved and forgiven. Armies of angels and the very presence of God surround you as you walk into every situation.

Strive to listen for God's answers to you. You may not hear it clearly at first.

5 ***Remember that the Savior wants what is best for you*** and will work on your behalf to accomplish it. The Holy Spirit continually intercedes for you in the very throne room of the Father! Consider the cloud of faithful witnesses, the believers who have already run and finished the race of faith. Their lives testify to the fact that the Lord never failed them, and he won't fail you.

6 ***Fix your eyes on Jesus as you throw off any sin*** that entangles you. Consider Jesus, who endured so much in his life just so you won't grow weary and lose heart in your own life.

7 ***Know people are praying for you.*** If you don't have that confidence in your own family, ask your spiritual family to pray for you. Give those you trust your specific prayer requests, and let them know you will pray for their specific requests.

8 ***Look for the good in every situation.*** Ask questions like these: How can God use this for the growth of his kingdom? How can someone be blessed through this? How is God working here? How can God use me in this situation? What response does he want from me? You may not always hear the answers clearly at first, but strive to listen for them, remembering that sometimes God speaks in a still, small voice. Also, realize that asking those questions is the easy part; having the disciplined patience to listen for the answers is more difficult. It won't do much good to ask unless you truly seek a response.

In some biblical translations, the very command "fear not" occurs regularly and insistently. That means you can go forward with confidence. God goes with you and leads the way. Fear not!

seek

The man who
graduates today
and
stops learning
tomorrow
is *uneducated*
the day after.

~ Newton D. Baker

Yet, O LORD, you are our Father.
We are the clay, you are the potter;
we are all the work of your hand.

~ Isaiah 64:8

The LORD your God is with you . . .
he will rejoice over you with singing.

~ Zephaniah 3:17

I thank my God
every time I remember you.
In all my prayers for all of you,
I always pray with joy
because of your partnership in the gospel
from the first day until now,
being confident of this,
that he who began a good work in you
will carry it on to completion
until the day of Christ Jesus.

~Philippians 1:3-6

The Unfinished Symphony

in the Key of Dee . . .

I *f you're reading this,* it means you're alive, which means God isn't finished with you yet! You have reached a major milestone in your life with his help, but he has even more in mind for you. I can't tell you all the details, but he knows them. He will reveal them to you in his perfect time.

Our plans are out of harmony with God's will.

Our lives are like an unfinished symphony. The composer of the music knows the ending, but those in the orchestra or the audience do not. The unfinished symphony of our lives is in the "key of dee . . . Lord's hands." He holds our lives in the palm of his hands.

Sometimes we won't understand the individual notes in the symphony. Our plans are out of harmony with God's will. Our sinful choices and the results of our sins are not in 'a-chord' with God's ways. But God can take the notes of triumph and even tragedy and from them create in our lives a masterpiece of beautiful music.

*I*n the coming years, you will hear many definitions of success. The world will scream to you about attaining success. But remember, the only "success" God calls you to is to be found in exercising the sweet gift of faith he gave you. And even in that you don't need to be successful because God yearns to be your help in times of trouble. In fact, Scripture never uses the word "successful," and God's definition of success differs radically from that of the world.

SO, WHAT DOES IT MEAN TO SET OUT
ON A PATH OF FAITHFULNESS—
THE KIND OF SUCCESS THAT HONORS GOD?

1) PUT GOD FIRST IN YOUR LIFE.

2) BE HUMBLE, GIVING GOD ALL GLORY.

3) WORK HARD.

4) BE TEACHABLE.

5) SEEK AND FOLLOW GOD'S WILL.

Speaking of Scripture, rejoice in this truth, truth that covers your unfinished life:

. . . he who began a good work in you will carry it on to completion until the day of Christ Jesus!

(Philippians 1:6)

Graduation isn't the end! Our God is in the business of completing what he begins—and he does it with the glue of his grace. He knew you before you were born. He formed you in your mother's womb. He hears your every thought and your every word, even before you think or speak them. He brought you a new life through a Spirit-created faith, re-birthed you through his life-creating Word, and baptized you into his family.

> *The Lord has brought your life to a great crescendo—your graduation!*

The Lord has brought your life to a great crescendo—your graduation! Congratulations on this achievement! But he's not finished. The song of your life isn't complete. He has more instrumentation to add, a series of trills and spills, notes of praise and of angelic choruses, until one day, at just the right moment, the grand finale! Only the final note isn't truly final, for the symphony will continue in heaven on perfect pitch with an unending chord of praise to the Master Teacher, the Ultimate Conductor, the world's Savior!

Let the celebratory music continue . . . and never end!

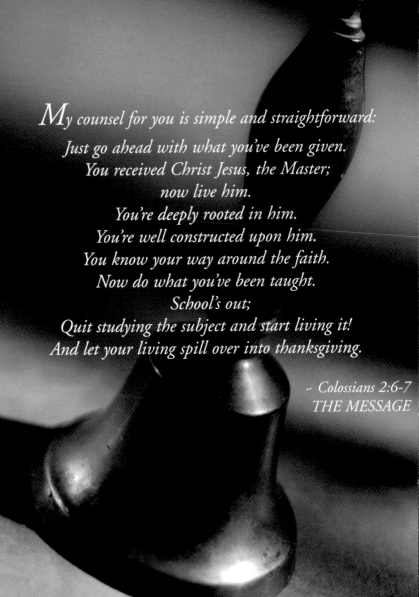

My counsel for you is simple and straightforward:
Just go ahead with what you've been given.
You received Christ Jesus, the Master;
now live him.
You're deeply rooted in him.
You're well constructed upon him.
You know your way around the faith.
Now do what you've been taught.
School's out;
Quit studying the subject and start living it!
And let your living spill over into thanksgiving.

~ Colossians 2:6-7
THE MESSAGE

Key Gifts of Grace from God:

A Journaling Resource

Who are the people God has used in my life to shape me spiritually?

How might these people impact my future spiritual growth as I move beyond the graduation tassel?

Holy Bible

*There's nothing like the written
Word of God for showing you the way to
salvation through faith in Christ Jesus.
Every part of Scripture is God-breathed and
useful one way or another –
showing us truth,
exposing our rebellion,
correcting our mistakes,
training us to live God's way.
Through the Word we are put together
and shaped up
for the tasks God has for us.*

*~ 2 Timothy 3:15b-17
THE MESSAGE*

"For I know the plans I have for you," declares the LORD, "plans to prosper you and not to harm you, plans to give you a hope and a future."

Jeremiah 29:11

Blessed is he whose transgressions are forgiven, whose sins are covered . . . I acknowledged my sin to you and did not cover up my iniquity. I said, "I will confess my transgressions to the LORD"—and you forgave the guilt of my sin.

Psalm 32:1,5

Your word is a lamp to my feet and a light for my path.

Psalm 119:105

God is our refuge and strength, an ever-present help in trouble.

Psalm 46:1

God's
Grace-filled
Words *for*
Tassel-Free Living

*Trust in the L*ORD *with all your heart and lean not on your own understanding; in all your ways acknowledge him, and he will make your paths straight.*

Proverbs 3:5-6

[Jesus said,] "… And surely I will be with you always, to the very end of the age."

Matthew 28:20

Jesus answered, "Everyone who drinks this water will be thirsty again, but whoever drinks the water I give him will never thirst. Indeed, the water I give him will become in him a spring of water welling up to eternal life."

John 4:13-14

[Jesus said,] "Peace I leave with you; my peace I give you. I do not give to you as the world gives. Do not let your hearts be troubled and do not be afraid."

John 14:27

[Jesus said,] "But seek first [the heavenly Father's] kingdom and his righteousness, and all these things will be given to you as well."

Matthew 6:33

For I am convinced that neither death nor life, neither angels nor demons, neither the present nor the future, nor any powers, neither height nor depth, nor anything else in all creation, will be able to separate us from the love of God that is in Christ Jesus our Lord.

Romans 8:38-39

The LORD your God is with you, he is mighty to save. He will take great delight in you, he will quiet you with his love, he will rejoice over

More God's Grace-filled Words for Tassel-Free Living

I am not ashamed of the Gospel, because it is the power of God for the salvation of everyone who believes … .

Romans 1:16

Jesus answered, "I am the way and the truth and the life. No one comes to the Father except through me."

John 14:6

… the fruit of the Spirit is love, joy, peace, patience, kindness, goodness, faithfulness, gentleness and self-control. Against such things there is no law.

Galatians 5:22-23

[Jesus said,] "For God so loved the world that he gave his one and only Son, that whoever believes in him shall not perish but have eternal life."

John 3:16

... Jesus said, "I am the light of the world. Whoever follows me will never walk in darkness, but will have the light of life."

John 8:12

Therefore, there is now no condemnation for those who are in Christ Jesus ... .

Romans 8:1

Jesus said ... , "I am the resurrection and the life. He who believes in me will live, even though he dies; and whoever lives and believes in me will never die ... ."

John 11:25-26

And we know that in all things God works for the good of those who love him, who have been called according to his purpose.

Romans 8:28

MORE God's
Grace-filled Words
for Tassel-Free *Living*

. . . Be faithful, even to the point of death, and I will give you the crown of life.

Revelation 2:10

I can do everything through [Christ] who gives me strength.

Philippians 4:13

For it is by grace you have been saved, through faith—and this not from yourselves, it is the gift of God—not by works, so that no one can boast.

Ephesians 2:8-9

Cast all your anxiety on him because he cares for you.

1 Peter 5:7

More of God's Grace-filled Words

for Tassel-Free Living

(Write in those passages that have been a special blessing in your life)

Family and Friends Who Celebrated My Graduation with Me

Special Events, Gifts, and Other Memories from Graduation Day

Special Events, Gifts, and Other Memories from Graduation Day *continued*

Special Events, Gifts, and Other Memories from Graduation Day *continued*

A Prayer for the Graduate

Gracious Lord,

Thank you for this time to celebrate! A graduation celebration wouldn't be possible without your gracious gifts.

The future isn't clear. I want to align my will with yours. Help me to trust in you rather than leaning on my own, limited understanding or the false promises of our culture. Give me confidence as I move into the future, knowing that everything that lies ahead has already passed through your thoughts; you see it all and want what is best for me. Help me to let you lead; help me to follow.

Thank you for gifting me with all the people, events, and experiences you have used to shape and form me into who I am today. Sustain my faith through your Word. As you have blessed me, use me to be a blessing to others in my life.

I love you, Lord. Thank you for your promise of grace and guidance for my life beyond the graduation tassel. Because of Jesus I can pray, Amen.

About the Author

The author, Tim Wesemann, has experienced his share of graduations—Salem Lutheran School, St. Paul Lutheran High School, Appalachian State University, and Concordia Seminary. A freelance writer and speaker, Tim lives in St. Louis, Missouri with his wife, Chiara; his children, Benjamin, Sarah, and Christopher; and an assortment of pets.

A former pastor, Tim has written several gift books for CTA as well as *Dr. Devo's Lickety-Split Devotions (Zonderkidz); Seasons under the Son (Concordia); and Being a Good Dad When You Didn't Have One Beacon Hill).*

Read more about his writing and speaking ministry at his website:
www.timwesemann.com